THE BOOK OF LEVITICUS

A Study Manual

by
CHARLES F. PFEIFFER

BAKER BOOK HOUSE
Grand Rapids 6, Michigan

Library of Congress Catalog Card Number: 57-14665

ISBN: 0-8010-6889-4

First printing, August 1957
Second printing, August 1963
Third printing, October 1967
Fourth printing, March 1971
Fifth printing, December 1973
Sixth printing, April 1977
Seventh printing, October 1980

PRINTED IN THE UNITED STATES OF AMERICA

TABLE OF CONTENTS

THE PURPOSE OF THIS MANUAL

Like the other volumes in this series, this *Study Manual for the Book of Leviticus* is designed to present the basic teaching of the Biblical book in an expanded outline form. Questions relative to the text of Leviticus and an evaluation of conflicting schools of interpretation do not enter the discussion; not that they are unimportant, but because they are foreign to the purpose of this Manual. Detailed information on critical problems may be secured by consulting the commentaries listed below.

The book of Leviticus is concerned with both law and grace. Its legal pronouncements affect every area of life, and concern attitudes and conduct with reference to God and man. Since God is infinitely holy, He demands holiness on the part of His people. Any uncleanness on the part of man interferes with fellowship with God, and renders service to God impossible. The law closes man's mouth before the heavenly tribunal, and declares man to be a sinner.

Grace appears in the book of Leviticus in that God, against whom man has sinned, has provided a way whereby broken fellowship may be restored. Provision for the presentation of acceptable sacrifices by an acceptable priesthood at an acceptable Sanctuary is one of the dominant notes of Leviticus. As the offended party, God has the right to declare the terms whereby the sinner may be reconciled. Those who attempt to come some other way are "thieves and robbers," and are subject to severe punishment (cf. Leviticus 10). With exact detail, the book of Leviticus indicates the way in which the Israelite, before the death of Christ, was to approach God.

Although the death of Christ put an end to the necessity for the sacrificial system described in Leviticus, the study of the book is more than of antiquarian interest. The New Testament Epistle to the Hebrews provides an inspired commentary on Leviticus. The concepts of sacrifice, priesthood, altar, and Tabernacle are used in the New Testament of Christ. To understand Him, and His atoning work for us, we must seek to understand those types and ceremonies which looked forward to Him, and which served as stars in the night, until the Sun of Righteousness arose.

Consonant with the purpose of this volume as a study guide, no attempt has been made to footnote comments or indicate sources of ideas presented. The following commentaries provide more detailed discussion of many of the points touched upon in this Guide:

Frederic Gardiner: "Leviticus" in *Lange's Commentary* (Scribner's) New York, 1876.

S. H. Kellogg: "The Book of Leviticus" in *The Expositor's Bible* (Armstrong & Son) New York, 1908.

C. F. Keil and F. Delitzsch: *Biblical Commentary on the Old Testament,* Vol. 2, The Pentateuch (reprint) (Eerdmans) Grand Rapids, 1949.

The following are brief, but helpful treatments of Leviticus in non-technical language:

Charles R. Erdman: *The Book of Leviticus* (Revell) New York, 1951.

Oswald T. Allis: "Leviticus" in Davidson, Stibbs, Kevan *The New Bible Commentary* (Eerdmans) Grand Rapids, 1953.

Oswald T. Allis: *God Spake by Moses* (Presbyterian and Reformed Publishing Co.) Philadelphia, 1951.

On the subject of Tabernacle, Priesthood, and Offerings, specialized works may be consulted. The following may be useful:

Patrick Fairbairn: *The Typology of Scripture* (Claxton) Philadelphia, 1867.

W. G. Moorehead: *Studies in the Mosaic Institutions* (United Brethren Publishing House) Dayton, Ohio, 1909.

Gustav Friederich Oehler: "Mosaism" in *Theology of the Old Testament,* Part I, (Funk & Wagnall) New York, 1883.

Geerhardus Vos: "The Mosaic Epoch of Revelation" in *Biblical Theology,* Part I, (Eerdmans) Grand Rapids, 1948.

INTRODUCTION

NAME. The third book in the Bible is called *vayikra,* "and he called," by the Jews, in accord with their custom of calling a book by its first word. The Septuagint Greek translation gave the book the title *Levitikon,* meaning Levitical (Book) because of the nature of its contents. This title was retained in the Latin Vulgate and is used in many modern translations.

PLACE IN THE BIBLE. The book of Genesis begins with a description of the origin of the universe and of mankind, a record of man's subsequent sin and expulsion from Paradise, and of the earliest epochs of human history. Beginning with Genesis 11, attention is focused upon God's revelation to and through Abraham and his "seed" or descendants. Genesis continues the history of the family of Abraham to the death of Joseph in Egypt.

After a lapse of years during which a Pharaoh "who knew not Joseph" came to the throne of Egypt, Exodus continues the story of God's dealings with the descendants of Abraham. Once a place of sustenance in a time of famine, now Egypt became a slave labor camp for oppressed Israelites.

Yet it is clear that God had not forgotten the covenant which He made with Abraham, Isaac, and Jacob. The prayers of His people are answered and a deliverer is provided in the person of Moses. As the climax of a series of judgments on Egypt, God used Moses in leading the people of Israel out of Egypt. The power of God was shown in the miraculous parting of the waters of the Red Sea to make the exodus possible, and the provision of manna from heaven and water from the rock to nourish and sustain the pilgrim people.

Exodus carries the history of Israel in its wilderness march as far as Mount Sinai. At Sinai, Israel entered into a solemn covenant with the Lord, in which Israel pledged its obedience to God's law, and the Lord covenanted to be the God of Israel, protecting Israel from its enemies, and blessing Israel as long as Israel would remain obedient to God's law. Much of subsequent Old Testament history is the record of Israel's sin in repeatedly breaking its covenant with God, and God's longsuffering and patience in raising up prophets to call His sinning people back to the paths of obedience and blessing.

Although disobedience to the law brought the wrath of God upon the sinner, God provided the institutions of priesthood and sacrifice whereby the transgressor could approach God and be assured of mercy. In order that this provision might not be misunderstood or abused, or lightly esteemed, God gave explicit directions concerning the circumstances under which the sinner might bring his sacrifice, the kinds of sacrifices that might be presented, and the qualifications of the priests who would approach God with the blood of the sacrifice on behalf of the sinner. Exodus 19-40 describes the giving of the law during the sojourn at the foot of Mt. Sinai, and the subsequent building of the Tabernacle, or Tent of Meeting. Here the Glory of the God of Israel dwelt above the mercy seat. In the court of the Tabernacle was an altar of brass which was the place of sacrifice. Beyond this altar, only the priests, the sons of Aaron, could go, and into the Holy of Holies, where the Glory of God was manifest, only the High Priest had access, and that only once a year on the solemn Day of Atonement.

The Book of Leviticus is concerned largely with the ministry of the priests ("the sons of Aaron") in the Tabernacle. Its solemn instructions cover every phase of the life of the Israelite. Its ordinances are designed to show forth the holiness of God, and the holiness He demands of His people. If that holiness appears to be external and ceremonial, it should be remembered that only in the Person of Christ can perfect holiness be found. Given in the day of types and shadows, Leviticus teaches the sinfulness of sin and is part of that law which was a schoolmaster to bring us to Christ.

Leviticus follows the account of the building of the Tabernacle (Exodus) and precedes the record of Israel's journey from Sinai to the land of promise (Numbers). While not historical in form, it is an important connecting link between Exodus and Numbers, indicating the law under which the priests labored, and the instructions which they were commanded to give to the people of Israel.

DATE AND AUTHORSHIP. With the other books of the Pentateuch, Leviticus has been traditionally ascribed to Moses by both Jewish and Christian scholars. With the rise of modern criticism, the antiquity of Leviticus was questioned. Dated in the period of 500-450 B.C., it was designated as "P" — the so-called

Priestly Code. Certain parts, notably the "Holiness Code" (chapters 18-20) were attributed to a somewhat earlier period.

The discoveries at Ras Shamra, ancient Ugarit, since 1929, have made necessary a scholarly reappraisal of the evidences for the date and authorship of the Pentateuch. Terminology in use in Ugarit during the 15th century B.C. is remarkably parallel to that of Leviticus. Terms such as "burnt offering," "whole burnt offering," "trespass offering," and "peace offering" appear in the Ugaritic literature. Arguments against the Mosaic authorship on the basis of language and religious development are no longer valid. It may be confidently affirmed that external evidence is in full accord with internal evidence for the Mosaic authorship of Leviticus.

OUTLINE OF THE BOOK OF LEVITICUS

Subject:

*The Way by which a Sinful Man may Approach God and
Continue in Fellowship with Him*

I. THE MEANS OF APPROACH TO GOD (Chaps. 1-16)

A. The Laws of Sacrifice (1-7)
   1. General Rules (1:1—6:7)

   a. Introduction (1:1-2)
     (1) The Divine Origin of Sacrifice (1:1)
     (2) The Voluntary Nature of These Sacrifices (1:2)
     (3) The Valuable Nature of These Sacrifices (1:2)

   b. The Burnt Offering (1:3-17)
     (1) Its Varieties
       (a) Of the Herd (1:3)
       (b) Of the Flock (1:10)
       (c) Of Fowl (1:14)
     (2) Its Ritual
       (a) Presentation (1:3) ⎫
       (b) Identification (1:4) ⎬ The Offerer's Part
       (c) Killing the Victim (1:5) ⎭
       (d) Sprinkling the Blood (1:5) ⎫
       (e) Preparing the Altar (1:7) ⎬ The Priest's Part
       (f) Washing and Burning the Sacrifice (1:9) ⎭
     (3) Its Purpose
       (a) Acceptance and Atonement (1:3, 4)
       (b) Consecration (1:9, 13, 17)

   c. Meal Offering (2)
     (1) Its Varieties
       (a) Unbaked Flour (2:1)
       (b) Baked Loaves or Cakes (2:4-11)
       (b) Green Ears of Corn (Wheat) (2:12-16)
     (2) Its Materials
       (a) Materials included
         Fine Flour (2:1)
         Oil (2:1)
         Frankincense (2:1)
         Salt (2:13)

      (b) Materials excluded
          Leaven (2:11)
          Honey (2:11)
   (3) Its Ritual
      (a) Presentation (2:2, 8)
      (b) Burning of the "Memorial" (2:2, 9, 16)
      (c) Eating by the Priests (2:3, 10)

d. Peace Offering (3)
   (1) Its Varieties
      (a) Of the Herd (3:1)
      (b) Of the Flock (3:6)
      (c) A Goat (3:12)
   (2) Its Ritual
      (a) Presentation (3:1)
      (b) Identification (3:2)
      (c) Killing the Victim (3:2)
      (d) Sprinkling the Blood (3:2)
      (e) Burning the Fat Portions on the Altar (3:3-5)
      (f) Setting Apart a Portion for the Priests (7:31)
      (g) The Remainder Eaten by the Worshipper
           (7:15-18)

e. Sin Offering (4:1—5:13)
   (1) Its Application (4:1)
   (2) Its Grades
      (a) For the High Priest (4:3)
      (b) For the Whole Congregation (4:13)
      (c) For the Ruler (4:22)
      (d) For the Private Citizen (4:27)
   (3) Its Ritual
      (a) Presentation (4:4)
      (b) Identification (4:4)
      (c) Killing the Victim (4:4)
      (d) Sprinkling the Blood:
          (1) Before the Veil in the Tabernacle
             (4:6, 17) and on the Horns of the Altar
             of Incense (4:7, 18)
                    or
          (2) On the Horns of the Altar of Burnt Of-
             fering (4:25, 30)
      (e) Pouring the Remaining Blood at the Base of
          the Altar of Burnt Offering (4:7, 18, 25, 30)

        (f) Burning the Fat Portions on the Altar (4:8-10)

        (g) Burning the Remainder of the Carcass in a Clean Place Outside the Camp (first two grades only) (4:11-12, 21).

    (4) Special Applicatons of Sin Offerings

        (a) Three Specific Signs

            (1) The Witness who Refused to Testify (5:1)

            (2) Accidental Ceremonial Defilement (5:2-3)

            (3) Idle Swearing (5:4)

        (b) Specific Offerings Prescribed in Such Cases

            (1) Female Sheep or Goat (5:6)

            (2) Two Turtledoves or Two Young Pigeons (5:7)

            (3) The Tenth Part of an Ephah of Fine Flour (5:11)

  f. Trespass Offering (5:14—6:7)

    (1) Its Occasion

        (a) Unintentional Trespass in the Things of God (5:14-19)

        (b) Unintentional Trespass against Man (5:20-26)

    (2) The Victim — a Ram (5:15, 18)

    (3) Its Ritual

        (a) Presentation of Ram to Priest (5:15, 25)

        (b) Make Restitution, plus an Added Fifth, to the Party Wronged (5:16, 23-24)

        (c) The Priest Offers the Sacrifice "to make atonement" for him (5:18, 26)

2. Special Instructions, Chiefly for the Priests (6:8—7:38)

  a. For Burnt Offerings (6:8-13)

  b. For Meal Offerings (6:14-23)

  c. For Sin Offerings (6:24-30)

  d. For Trespass Offerings (7:1-10)

  e. For Peace Offerings (7:11-34)

  f. The Divine Origin of the Laws (7:35-38)

B. Historical Section (8-10)

  1. The Consecration of the Priests (8)

    a. Introduction (8:1-5)

    b. Cleansing of Aaron and His Sons (8:6)

    c. Investiture of Aaron (8:7-9)

　　b. The Second Table of the Law　(19:9-18)
　　　　(1) Consideration for the Poor　(19:9-10)
　　　　(2) Prohibition against Robbery and Deceit　(19:11)
　　　　(3) Prohibition against False Swearing　(19:12)
　　　　(4) Prohibition against Oppression　(19:13)
　　　　(5) Care for the Helpless　(19:14)
　　　　(6) Righteous Judgments　(19:15)
　　　　(7) Warning against "Tale-bearing"　(19:16)
　　　　(8) Summary of the Second Table of the Law
　　　　　　(19:17-18)
　　c. Various ordinances　(19:19-29)
　　　　(1) Prohibition against "Hybrids"　(19:19)
　　　　(2) Sin of a Betrothed Bondmaid　(19:20-22)
　　　　(3) The "First-Fruit" of the Trees of Canaan
　　　　　　(19:23-25)
　　　　(4) Abstention from Heathen Rites　(19:26-29)
　　d. Concluding injunctions　(19:30-37)
　　　　(1) Honor to the Sabbath and the Sanctuary　(19:30)
　　　　(2) Avoid "familiar spirits" and "wizards"　(19:31)
　　　　(3) Honor the Aged　(19:32)
　　　　(4) Deal Kindly with the Stranger　(19:33-34)
　　　　(5) The Standard of Righteousness　(19:35-36)
　　　　(6) Summary — The Reason for Obedience　(19:37)

4. Punishment for Unholiness　(20)
　　a. Molech Worship　(20:1-5)
　　b. Consorting with Wizards and Necromancers　(20:6-8)
　　c. Cursing Parents　(20:9)
　　d. Sexual Crimes　(20:10-21)
　　e. Exhortation to Faithfulness　(20:22-26)
　　f. Warning against Unfaithfulness　(20:27)

B. Holiness on the Part of Priests, and Holiness of the Offerings
　　(21-22)

　　1. Avoidance of Contact with a Dead Body　(21:1-4)
　　2. Abstention from Heathen Practices　(21:5-6)
　　3. The Marriage of Priests　(21:7-8)
　　4. The Family of Priests　(21:9)
　　5. The High Priest　(21:10-15)
　　6. Priests with Physical Blemishes　(21:16-24)
　　7. Priestly Separation from Ceremonial Uncleanness
　　　　(22:1-10)

I *The Means of Approach to God* (Chaps. 1-16).

A. The Laws of Sacrifice (Chaps. 1-7).

1. (1:1—6:7) General Rules.

a. (1:1-2) Introduction.

(1) The Divine Origin of Sacrifice (1:1). At Mount Sinai, God gave His law through Moses. That law makes manifest the holiness of God and declares His righteous demands upon sinful men. With the law, however, God gave witness concerning His grace. Here He reveals through Moses the way by which sinful man may be restored to a place of fellowship with God — through atoning sacrifice.

(2) The Voluntary Nature of These Sacrifices (1:2). Certain sacrifices are prescribed, and obedience to God demands that they be presented at the time and in the manner designated. Such, for example, are the sacrifices prescribed for the Day of Atonement (Leviticus 16). The sacrifices first described, however, are not assigned to stated occasions, but are voluntarily presented by individuals conscious of having sinned against God, and standing in need of atonement.

(3) The Valuable Nature of These Sacrifices (1:2). Although provision is made for the very poor, the animals presented in sacrifice are, as a rule, costly. Atonement is not cheap. God gave "His only begotten Son." The usual offering in the Old Testament economy was "of the herd, or of the flock" — domesticated rather than wild.

b. (1:3-17) The Burnt Offering *('olah)*. The Hebrew word translated "burnt offering" means, literally, "that which goes up." The Burnt Offering is distinguished from the other offerings in that all of the flesh is consumed on the altar. For this reason it is called the "whole burnt offering" *(kalil)*. Burnt Offerings were offered in the most remote antiquity. The offerings of Abel, Noah, Abraham, and the patriarchs of Israel fall into this category. Sacrifices at the altar each morning and each evening give us the term "Continual Burnt Offering" (Exodus 29:42; Numbers 28-29). The Brazen Altar in the court of the Tabernacle is sometimes called the "Altar of Burnt Offering."

(1) Its Varieties (1:3, 10, 14).

(a) Of the Herd. (1:3). The most costly Burnt Offering was that which came from the herd of cattle. It must be a male, as the stronger sex, and without blemish, as symbolic of the perfection which God demands. That which is blemished, and unfit for human use, should never be offered to God.

(b) Of the Flock (1:10). Sheep or goats are of less financial value than cattle. They are acceptable Burnt Offerings, however, if the choice is of an unblemished male.

(c) Of Fowl (1:14). For those unable to present more costly offerings, provisions is made for the presentation of the turtle-dove (abundant in spring and summer and easily caught) and pigeons (wild in all seasons and difficult to catch, but bred from early times). Thus no one need allow poverty to keep him from making his offerings to the Lord.

(2) Its Ritual. The law prescribes both the acceptable sacrifice and the means by which it is to be presented. The first three elements in the ritual are performed by the offerer, after which the priest performs certain prescribed rites.

(a) Presentation (1:3). The offerer is directed to bring his offering to the door of the Tabernacle. The Tabernacle was not a public meeting place, but the place in which the Levitical priests performed the services prescribed for them. The lay Israelite never entered the Tabernacle itself. He came as far as the Brazen Altar, just inside the door of the Tabernacle court. In presenting his sacrifice there he acknowledged his sin and his trust in the divinely appointed means of expiation.

(b) Identification (1:4). The offerer was directed to lay his hand on the head of the sacrificial victim. The significance of this action has been the subject of much discussion. In the ritual for the Day of Atonement the laying on of hands is associated with the confession of sin (16:21), preliminary to sending the scapegoat into the wilderness symbolically to bear away the sins of the people. Here it appears that the animal is designated as the substitute for the sinning Israelite, and the sinner's guilt is symbolically transferred to the victim.

(c) Killing the Victim (1:5). This is the last act of the offerer. The victim takes the place of the sinner. "The wages of sin is death" (Romans 6:23). Bearing, in symbol, the sin of the offerer, the offering is slain.

(d) Sprinkling the Blood (1:5). After the victim has been slain, the ministry of the priest begins. He sprinkles the blood on the altar, indicating that the sacrifice is made to God for the purpose of expiation. The rendering "and dash the blood round against the altar" (Jewish Publication Society Translation) expresses the action of the priest more vividly than does the usual translation, "sprinkle."

(e) Preparing the Altar. (1:7). It was the responsibility of the priests to provide wood and maintain fire on the altar. The ascent to the altar was at the south side, the ashes were piled at the east side, the killing of the victim took place at the north side (cf. 1:11). The west side of the altar faced the Tabernacle.

(f) Washing and Burning the Sacrifice (1:9). After all preliminaries were attended to, the priest burned the entire sacrifice. In the symbol of the smoke rising heavenward God is seen as accepting with pleasure the prescribed sacrifice, offered in an attitude of faith.

(3) **Its Purpose.**

(a) Atonement or Acceptance (1:3, 4). Note that the rendering "of his own voluntary will" in the King James Version should be rendered, "that he may be accepted." The sacrifice is offered because sin has brought a condition of estrangement between God and the offerer. Man has sinned, but God has provided the remedy in an atoning sacrifice. Atonement is, literally, a covering *(kaper)*. The offerer is sheltered from the penalty which is his due as a sinner. In anthropomorphic language, God looks from heaven and sees not the sinner in his sin, but the covering, the atonement which He has provided. In Christ the believer has full atonement, and is "accepted in the beloved."

(b) Consecration (1:9, 13, 17). The offering is termed "a sweet savour unto the Lord." The offering is given from a heart of love and, in the case of the Burnt Offering, wholly presented to God. From one point of view the sacrifice died on the altar because "the wages of sin is death." From another point of view, the sacrifice died because the offerer desired to present his very best to God. Both of these truths find expression in the death of Christ, "made sin for us" and offering Himself "for us an offering and a sacrifice to God for a sweet-smelling savour" (Ephesians 5:2).

c.   **(2:1-16) The Meal Offering (A.V. "Meat Offering")** *(minḥah).* A gift or present of any kind may be termed a *minḥah.* Presents offered to nobles or kings are so designated, as when Ehud brought a *minḥah* to Eglon, king of Moab (Judges 3:15). In the Levitical offerings a *minḥah* is a gift to God of the daily food of the people. It appears always to have been offered as an adjunct to a bloody sacrifice (cf. Leviticus 23:18; Ezra 7:17). The word is used of the offerings of both Cain and Abel in Genesis 4. Cain's failure to present a bloody sacrifice, in accord with God's revealed will, may be the ground for the conclusion that his offering was without faith (Hebrews 11:4, 6).

(1) **Its Varieties.** As in the case of the Burnt Offering, the Meal Offering could be offered in one of three forms, designed, no doubt, to meet the needs of the people.

(a) **Unbaked Flour (2:1).** The word *soleth* is used of the finest and purest of flour. Wheat appears to have been used.

(b) **Baked Loaves or Cakes (2:4-11).** Oil is either an ingredient in the cakes, or they are anointed or smeared with oil.

(c) **Green Ears of Corn (i.e. Wheat) (2:12-16).** The grain is parched, or roasted as an offering of first-fruits to the Lord. It is not burned on the altar.

(2) **Its Materials.** Specific directions are given as to what is included and what is excluded from the Meal Offering.

(a) **Materials Included in the Offering.**

(i) **Fine Flour (2:2).** The principal ingredient of the Meal Offering was fine flour, corresponding to the "without blemish" of the animal sacrifices. Only the best is suitable for worship and sacrifice.

(ii) **Oil (2:2).** Oil was added to all Meal Offerings. Oil played an important part in the Old Testament economy for it was used in the anointing of priests, kings, and, in certain cases, prophets. The oil used was that of the olive.

(iii) Frankincense (2:2). Frankincense was a resinous gum, probably imported from Southwestern Arabia. It was not mixed with the flour and oil, but so added that it might be removed with the "handful" which was to be burned as the "memorial" on the altar.

(iv) Salt (2:13). Salt was the preservative of the ancient world. A "covenant of salt" is a perpetual covenant. The purifying and preserving principle of salt must be present in each sacrifice.

(b) Materials Excluded from the Offering.

(i) Leaven (2:4, 5, 11). The process of fermentation, brought about by means of leaven, was looked upon as akin to corruption. As such it was unsuitable for the Lord's altar, although it was continually offered to heathen deities. Leaven was permitted in those offerings which were designated for the priests in Israel, as in the Peace Offering (7:13, 14).

(ii) Honey (2:11). The honey here mentioned probably is to be identified with the juice of fruit, particularly dates, rather than the honey of bees. This, like leaven, would be associated with fermentation.

(3) Its Ritual. The rituals for the various offerings have much in common. In each case there is a presentation by the offerer followed by certain priestly ministrations.

(a) Presentation (2:2, 8). The offering is prepared in advance by the offerer and presented to the priest.

(b) Burning (2:2, 9, 16). The priest was instructed to take a handful of the offering, including all the frankincense, and burn it on the altar. This is called the "Memorial" (*Azkarah*), and is described as a "sweet savour" unto the Lord. The Greek equivalent of the *Azkarah* (from the Septuagint) is used of the prayers and alms of Cornelius (Acts 10:4). The offerer is remembered before the throne of Grace on the basis of his offering.

(c) Eating (2:3, 10). That part of the offering which was not burned was termed "most holy" and designated for the priests. This provision serves as a reminder of God's care for those whose lives are devoted to His service, and the solemn responsibility of the priest in his handling and appropriation of that which is "most holy."

d.   **(3:1-17)** The Peace Offering *(zebah shelamim).* The term *shelamim* is applied to those sacrifices which are concluded with a sacrificial meal. In the Burnt Offering the entire sacrifice is burned on the altar. The priests received portions of the Meal, Sin, and Trespass offerings. In the Peace Offering, however, the worshipper as well as the priest has the privilege of participating in the sacrificial meal. The Peace Offering is discussed in greater detail in Leviticus 7:11-38.

The Peace Offering is sometimes called the Thank Offering. While in all the offerings there is a recognition and consciousness of sin and the need of atonement, the Peace Offering stresses that fellowship which is the portion of the individual who is in a right relationship with God.

The Peace Offering appears to have invariably followed other sacrifices. This is true on the occasion of the consecration of Aaron and his sons (Leviticus 8), and the services of the Day of Atonement (Leviticus 16). Those sacrifices which set forth the concept of atonement from sin logically precede those which stress the joy of fellowship in holy things.

(1)   Its Varieties **(3:1, 6, 12).**

(a)   A Victim of the Herd **(3:1).** As in all offerings, the sacrificial victim must be flawless, "without blemish." Unlike the Burnt Offering which required that the victim be a male, the Peace Offering may be either male or female.

(b)   A Victim of the Flock **(3:6).** A male or female lamb would provide a suitable Peace Offering. This must also be without blemish.

(c)   A Goat **(3:12).** Considerable latitude is allowed in the choice of victims for the Peace Offering. It may be observed, however, that no mention is made of the offerings of the poor — turtle-doves and pigeons. This is doubtless because of the nature of the offering. The fowl could not be divided so as to allow the worshipper to use a portion as a festive meal. The poor would doubtless be invited to share the Peace Offerings of their more wealthy friends.

(2)   Its Ritual.

(a)   Presentation **(3:1, 7, 12).** The offerer personally presents the animal designated for the Peace Offering to the priest. The mercies of God are publicly announced in this act which was performed at the door of the Tabernacle.

(b) Identification (3:2, 8, 13). As in all of the bloody sacrifices, the worshipper symbolically placed his hands on the head of the sacrifice. The very blessing of fellowship, enjoyed in the celebration of the Peace Offering, was achieved through the death of a Substitute.

(c) Killing the Victim (3:2, 8, 13). Life comes from death. The victim must die before he can feed anyone. So Christ, crucified, is the bread for needy mankind.

(d) Sprinkling the Blood (3:2, 8, 13). The application of the blood, as in the other bloody offerings, is the work of the priest. Sinful man needs a Mediator to represent him before God. The Levitical priest served in this capacity until Christ, a "priest forever after the order of Melchizedek," became the Mediator through whom the blessings of God are applied to man.

(e) Burning the Fat Portions on the Altar (3:3-5, 9-11, 14-17). Peace offerings were preceded as a rule by the Burnt Offerings which were offered daily. The fat portions of the Peace Offering were placed upon the already burning Burnt Offering (cf. 6:5, 9:14).

   The fat was esteemed the richest and best part of the animal. As such it was offered to God: "All the fat is the Lord's" (3:16). Neither fat nor blood could be eaten by the Israelite who was obedient to the Mosaic law (3:17).

   We are told that the "fat tails" of Syrian sheep often weigh as much as fifteen pounds. This is the appendage referred to in 3:9 as "the whole rump" in the Authorized Version. It consists of an excrescence of fat and marrow from which the true tail hangs, and formed part of the fat of the Peace Offering that was burned on the altar as the Lord's portion.

(f) Setting Apart a Portion for the Priests (7:31-36). The breast and the right thigh were set apart for Aaron and his sons. The breast was used as a wave offering. The priest moved the wave offering to and fro, toward and away from the altar in token of its dedication to God. Instead of being burned, however, it was given to the priests as a part of their portion of the Peace Offering.

(g) The Remainder Eaten by the Worshipper (7:15-18). All that
remained of the victim, after the Lord and the priests had
their portion, belonged to the offerer. He might invite his
friends and the Levites to share the feast with him. Normally
all of the flesh of the Peace Offering should be eaten on the
day on which the offering was made. When the offering was
in fulfillment of a vow, the flesh might be kept one additional day, after which it must be burned.

e. (4:1—5:13) The Sin Offering *(hata)*. Sin and Trespass Offerings were named for the purposes for which they apply —
the expiation of the guilt of sin and trespasses against God
and man.
   The Hebrew word *hata* may be translated "sin" or "sin
offering" depending on the context. Like the Greek
hamartano, the Hebrew *hata* conveys the idea of missing
the mark (cf. Judges 20:16). Since all "come short of the
glory of God" sin offerings are provided for each segment
of society.

(1) Its Application (4:2). The Sin Offering applies only to those
who sin "through ignorance" or inadvertence. While this
might appear to seriously restrict the area of application of
the Sin Offering, such is not the case. Sins committed
"through ignorance" *(bishegagah)* are sins arising from
human infirmity, or the weakness of "flesh and blood."
Manslaughter without malice is so designated (Numbers
35:11-23). The opposite of the sin "through ignorance" is
that "with a high hand," i.e. in calculated defiance of God.
Those guilty of such sins were cut off without mercy (Numbers 15:27-31). In the final analysis, God alone knows
whether a sin is committed "through ignorance" or "with a
high hand."

(2) Its Grades. God has but one standard of morality. Responsibility differs, however, in proportion to the privileges and
positions entrusted to the individual. The man with ten
talents has a responsibility beyond that of the man entrusted
with one. No person is so obscure that his sin is overlooked.
None is so prominent that his sin is condoned.

(a) For the High Priest (4:3). The High Priest has the responsibility of representing the nation before God. His sin, directly
or indirectly, brings guilt upon the people. Through sin he

may be disqualified from offering the sacrifice which atones for the people's sins. His counsel may be such as to lead the people astray. The Sin Offering prescribed for the High Priest is the largest of the sacrificial animals, a young bullock, without blemish.

(b) For the Whole Congregation (4:13). There were occasions in the history of Israel when the law of God was neglected to the point that the nation as a whole was guilty of sin. Such was the situation when the "Law of the Lord" was found in the Temple in the days of Josiah (II Kings 22:3– 23:25). The neglect of specific commands, such as that for the observance of the Sabbatical year (II Chronicles 36:21), and the neglect of tithes and offerings were sins of the nation as a whole. In such cases the prescribed Sin Offering was the same as that for the High Priest, a young bullock.

(c) For the Ruler (4:22). As an individual, the responsibility of the ruler is second to that of the High Priest. Although not concerned with "holy things" to the extent of the High Priest, he has been chosen of God for a place of trust, and is expected to set an example of godliness before the people who are subject to him. The Sin Offering prescribed for the ruler is a male goat. The ritual of offering, likewise, differs from that prescribed for the High Priest.

(d) For the Private Citizen (4:27-35). The individual member of the Israelite community was responsible for living a life of obedience to God's revealed will. When aware of his need for a Sin Offering he was directed to bring a female goat or a lamb. The ritual was the same as that for the ruler.

(3) Its Ritual.

(a) Presentation (4:4, 15, 23, 28). The individual who had sinned was obliged to present the prescribed sacrifice at the altar. In the case of the whole congregation's sin it appears that the community gathered at the door of the Tabernacle.

(b) Identification (4:4, 15, 24, 29). As in the other animal sacrifices, the offerer placed his hand on the head of the victim. When the entire congregation had sinned, the elders acted on behalf of all the people.

(c) Killing the Victim (4:4, 15, 24, 29). The victim is killed by the offerer or, presumably, by the elders in the case of the sin of the entire congregation.

(d) Sprinkling the Blood. The rite of sprinkling the blood differs according to the grade of the Sin Offering.

(1) Before the Veil in the Tabernacle and on the Horns of the Altar of Incense (4:6-7, 17-18).

In the case of offerings for the sins of the High Priest and the entire congregation the priest took the blood of sacrifice into the Tabernacle. Seven times the blood was sprinkled before the veil which separated the Holy Place from the Holy of Holies. Blood was also applied to the horns of the altar of incense in the Holy Place.

(2) On the Horns of the Altar of Burnt Offering (4:25, 30). In offerings for a ruler or a private citizen, the priest did not take the blood into the Tabernacle, but applied it to the horns of the brazen altar of Burnt Offering in the Tabernacle court.

(e) Pouring the Remaining Blood at the Base of the Altar of Burnt Offering (4:7, 18, 25, 30). The blood that was not specifically applied to the veil, golden altar of incense, or brazen altar of Burnt Offering, was poured out at the base of the altar of Burnt Offering in the Tabernacle court.

(f) Burning the Fat Portions on the Altar (4:8-10, 19, 26, 31). The fat portions, deemed the best part of the offering, were burned by the priest on the altar of Burnt Offering, as in the case of the Peace Offering.

(g) Burning the Remainder of the Carcass in a Clean Place Outside the Camp (4:11-12, 21). In the offerings for the High Priest and for the whole congregation we are told that the remainder of the carcass of the victim was carried to a ceremonially clean place outside the camp of Israel, and there burned. The author of Hebrews alluded to this part of the ritual in speaking of the sufferings of Christ "outside the camp" (Hebrews 13:10-13). In the ritual for the ruler and the individual member no mention is made of burning "outside the camp."

(4) Special Applications of Sin Offerings. In addition to the general application of the Sin Offering to transgressions committed by the various segments of Israelite society, three specific sins are mentioned with their appropriate offerings.

(a) Three Specific Sins (5:1-4).

(1) The Witness Who Refused to Testify (5:1). At the public investigation of a crime, qualified witnesses were asked to come forward and tell what they knew concerning the matter. A qualified witness who neglected to give his testimony was guilty of sin, and needed an atoning sacrifice.

(2) Accidental Ceremonial Defilement (5:2-3). The person who unknowingly touches the unclean carcass of a beast, or comes into contact with ceremonial uncleanness of man is in need of cleansing. When such an individual learns that he has become ceremonially defiled, he is expected to provide the appropriate sacrifice.

(3) Idle Swearing (5:4). An oath thoughtlessly uttered was regarded as sinful. The scope of the oath, "to do evil or to do good" implies "to do anything." Opposites in Scripture frequently signify totality. Any idle oath is sinful.

(b) Specific Offerings Prescribed in Such Cases (5:6-13).

(1) A Female Sheep or Goat (5:6). A female sheep or goat is prescribed as the Sin Offering for the specific sins named in verses 1-4. The offering follows confession (5:5), and is brought to the priest to be used as an atoning sacrifice.

(2) Two Turtledoves, or Two Young Pigeons (5:7). The individual who cannot afford a sheep or goat may satisfy the law of sacrifice by bringing turtle-doves, or pigeons, one for a Sin Offering and the other for a Burnt Offering. They are prepared by the priest for sacrifice, and are accepted for the atonement of the guilty party.

(3) The tenth part of an ephah of fine flour (5:11). If the sinner cannot afford even the turtle-doves or pigeons, he may present the tenth part of an ephah of fine flour, wthout oil or frankincense, as his Sin Offering. The quantity specified is the equivalent of a day's food. The "memorial" part of the flour is burned on the altar by the priest, as in the Meal Offering, and the rest assigned to the priest as food. Even this least expensive offering guarantees the acceptance of the repentant sinner before the throne of Grace.

f. (5:14—6:7) The Trespass Offering *(asham)*. The *asham*, rendered "Trespass Offering" or "Guilt Offering," emphasizes the idea of the harm done by the transgressor of the law, whereas the Sin Offering emphasizes the sin committed. The

distinctive feature of the Trespass Offering is the demand
that amends be made for the harm done by adding a fifth
(a double tithe) to the amount paid in restitution for a
fraud committed against God or man.

(1)   Its Occasion.

(a)   Unintentional Trespass in the Things of God. (5:14-19).
The Israelite recognized that the Lord had certain legal
rights to his person and property. Each member of the
community had solemnly pledged himself to a life of faithfulness to those obligations. When an Israelite violated the
rights of God "through error" (in contrast to wilfully vio-
lating the law) he was commanded to bring a Trespass
Offering and make restitution for the wrong done. The sin
might involve neglect or forgetfulness in the matter of first
fruits, tithes, or other prescribed offerings.

(b)   Unintentional Trespass against Man (5:20-26). Sins against
man are also trespasses against God, for the law of God
regulates human conduct in the relationships of man to
man as well as relationships between man and God. It is
not enough for man to make amends to the individual he
has defrauded. Sin is against God, and a Trespass Offering
is required.

(2)   The Victim (5:15, 18). The Trespass Offering is limited to
one sacrificial animal — "a ram without blemish out of the
flock" (5:15, 18, 6:6). The value of the ram is prescribed in
the Hebrew idiom *keseph shekalim* "money of shekels,"
which Jewish commentators have interpreted as meaning
that the ram must have the value of at least two shekels.
     The ram was a valuable offering, more valuable than the
ewe or the lamb, and much more valuable than the turtle-
dove or pigeon. Israel must learn that transgression is costly.
Yet the offering prescribed was not the costly bullock which
would have been out of reach for many.

(3)   Its ritual.

(a)   Presentation of Ram to the Priest (5:15, 25). The individual
who had committed the trespass was required to present
his ram of the required value to the priest. It was the responsibility of the priest to examine it, being sure it was
without blemish and of the proper value.

(b) Make Restitution, Plus an Added Fifth, to the Party Wronged **(5:16, 23-24)**. Because the trespass involved an invasion of the rights of God or a fellow man, restitution was demanded before atonement could be accomplished. To offset any gain which the transgressor had enjoyed during the period of his possession of that which was not rightly his, a fifth was added to the sum he was obliged to pay. In sins pertaining to the things of the Lord, payment was made to the priests (5:16), but where the transgression was against man, payment was made to the injured party (6:5).

(c) The Priest Offers the Sacrifice "to make atonement" for him **(5:18, 26)**. The blood of the Trespass Offering was sprinkled on the Altar of Burnt Offering (7:2) and the fat portions were burned on the altar (7:5), the remainder being eaten by the priests (7:6).

2. **(6:8—7:38)** Special Instructions, Chiefly for the Priests. The earlier discussion of the offerings was addressed to the Israelites as a whole (cf. 1:2). Beginning with 6:8 the regulations are addressed to "Aaron and his sons," or the Levitical priesthood. Further details are then given concerning the priestly ministry as it pertains to the five offerings discussed in 1:1—6:7.

a. **(6:8—13)** For Burnt Offerings. The earlier discussion of the Burnt Offering was in the context of individual offerings on the basis of individual guilt. Here the daily Burnt Offering is prescribed for all the people. The priest was ordered to array himself in his sacerdotal garments. The daily service consisted of two lambs, one offered at sunrise and the other at evening (cf. Exodus 29:38; Numbers 28:3). After the sacrifice, the priest was ordered to assume his ordinary garb and carry out the ashes.

The fire on the altar of Burnt Offering was to be kept burning perpetually. Wood was provided for the fire at the expense of the congregation.

b. **(6:14-23)** For Meal Offerings. In chapter 2, the people were given instructions concerning the nature of the Meal Offering. Here additional directions are given to the priests about the eating of the portions which belong to them and the treatment of that which is left.

A special provision is made for a continual Meal Offering for the priests. It is offered by Aaron, or his successor in office, each morning and each evening. Since it is offered for the priests, no part is eaten by them. It is wholly burned.

c.   **(6:24-30) For Sin Offerings.** Precise directions are given to the priests concerning the Sin Offering. All of the flesh of the Sin Offering except the fat became the portion of the officiating priest. All that touches it must be regarded as holy because of the sanctity of the offering. Unglazed earthenware vessels which would absorb some of the juices of the flesh boiled in them were broken.

An exception is made in the case of the Sin Offerings made for the High Priest (4:3, 12), the congregation as a whole (4:13-21), and the Sin Offerings of the Day of Atonement (16:27). Such Sin Offerings were not to be eaten by the priests, but were rather to be burned.

d.   **(7:1-10) For Trespass Offerings.** The law of the Trespass Offering is stated in detail in order to indicate clearly the Lord's portion in this sacrifice. It is stated that the portion of the priest in this offering is the same as in the Sin Offering. Everything except the Lord's portion goes to the priest.

e.   **(7:11-34) For Peace Offerings.** The Peace Offering is the one sacrifice in which the offerer is permitted to partake.

The Lord's portion is the fat which is burned on the altar. The breast and the right thigh are assigned to the priest. In the symbolism of the Peace Offering the worshipper gave these portions to God through the priest. The rest of the flesh became the portion of the worshipper.

If the sacrifice was a vow, or free-will offering, any remainder might be eaten on the second day. Thanksgiving offerings must be eaten on the day on which they are offered. Any remainder had to be burned. Friends and neighbors, especially the poor and needy, were normally invited to share the Peace Offering.

f.   **(7:35-38) The Divine Origin of the Laws.** Emphasis is placed on the fact that the law was given by God at Mt. Sinai and that a continuing provision is made for the sustenance of the priests by means of the sacred offerings.

B.   Historical Section (Chaps. 8-10).

1.   **(8) The Consecration of the Priests.** The commandment to appoint Aaron and his sons to the priesthood, with directions for the preparation of the official garments and for the consecration rite had been given with the instructions for the building and arrangement of the Tabernacle (Exodus 28:29; 40:9-16). The service could not be carried out until the law of the offerings had been given.

a.   **(8:1-5) Introduction.** The entire congregation was ordered to gather at the door of the Tabernacle for the solemn occasion of the anointing of Aaron and his sons.

b.   **(8:6) Cleansing.** Aaron and his sons were bathed in water, symbolic of the spiritual cleansing required of all who approach God.

c.   **(8:7-9) Investiture** (cf. Exodus 29). The putting on of official dress was symbolic of endowment with the grace required to discharge the duties of the priestly office. This included:

(1) The Tunic — an undercoat of white linen.

(2) The Girdle — a linen strip about five inches wide.

(3) The Robe — or overcoat, known as "the robe of the ephod," made of blue cloth with a border of pomegranates and golden bells in alternation.

(4) The Ephod — a dress of blue, purple, scarlet, and fine linen interwoven with gold (Exodus 28:6-8; 39:2-5). The front and back pieces of the ephod were fastened at the shoulder of the High Priest with onyx stones upon which were engraved the names of the twelve tribes (Exodus 28:9-14; 39:6-7).

(5) The Girdle — or band of the ephod was of the same material and colors as the ephod.

(6) The Breastplate — worn over the ephod, was also of the same material and colors as the ephod. It hung from the priest's shoulders by golden chains. Set in the breastplate were four rows containing twelve precious stones engraved with the names of the twelve tribes of Israel.

(7) The Urim and Thummim. These were placed in the folds of the breastplate. The exact nature of the Urim and Thummim (perhaps meaning "lights and perfections") is not known. They were used to determine the will of God in certain circumstances (cf. I Samuel 14:41-42; 28:6).

(8) The Mitre — or turban, a headdress of fine linen.

(9) "The Golden Plate, the Holy Crown" — a band of gold bound about the forehead of the High Priest, over the mitre. On it were engraved the words, "Holiness to the Lord."

d.   **(8:10-12)** The Anointing of the Tabernacle and Aaron.

(1)   The Tabernacle. The Tabernacle and its furniture were anointed and formally set apart for the sacred ministry for which they were made.

(2)   Aaron. For ordinary priests oil was smeared with the finger on the forehead. It was poured on Aaron's head, however, in token of his position as High Priest.

e.   **(8:13)** Investiture of Aaron's Sons. Coats, girdles, and mitre (turban) were placed on the sons of Aaron in setting them apart for the priesthood. That they were anointed is clear from Exodus 40:15.

f.   **(8:14-17)** The Sin Offering. As the mediator of the covenant, Moses officiated at the presentation of the first Sin Offering. A young bullock, the highest grade of Sin Offering, was presented. Moses placed blood on the horns of the altar of Burnt Offering. The rest of the blood was poured at the base of the altar. The fat of the offering was burned on the altar. The flesh, hide, and dung were burned outside the camp.

g.   **(8:18-21)** The Burnt Offering. Aaron and his sons placed their hands on the head of the ram designated for the Burnt Offering. Blood was applied to the altar after which the ram was wholly consumed as a Burnt Offering.

h.   **(8:22-29)** The Consecration Offering — A Peace Offering. In addition to the ram of the Burnt Offering, Aaron and his sons placed their hands on the head of a second ram, called the "ram of consecration," or, literally, "ram of filling." This is the ordination or installation service for the Aaronic priesthood.

The blood of the slain ram was applied to the right ear, right thumb, and right big toe of Aaron, after which the same ritual was applied to his sons. The remainder of the blood was applied to the altar.

Certain portions of the meal offering were placed over a

portion of the ram of the Consecration Offering, in the hands of Aaron and his sons, and the whole was waved "for a wave-offering before the Lord." Afterward the offerings were wholly consumed on the altar of Burnt Offering. In this ceremony the house of Aaron was formally charged with responsibility for the offering of the sacrifices. In the wave offering the sacrifice was formally given to God, and received back from Him. The priests who now handled the sacrifices were set apart for their ministry by Moses, the mediator of the covenant which God established with Israel at Sinai.

i. (8:30) The Sanctification of Aaron and His Sons. A mixture of anointing oil and blood was sprinkled on the person and garments of Aaron and his sons.

j. (8:31-32) Eating the Sacrifice. The newly ordained priests were instructed to boil the flesh of the ram of consecration at the door of the Tabernacle and eat it there with the bread from the basket of consecration offerings. In this meal the intimacy of the priests with the Lord as ministers in His house was stressed. As servants of God, they were fed at His altar. Anything not eaten by the priests was burned.

k. (8:33-36) Abiding in the Tabernacle. The consecration ceremonies were repeated each day for a week. Aaron and his sons were commanded to remain in the Tabernacle until this solemn week of consecration had ended.

2. (9) Entrance of Aaron and His Sons on Their Office. Following the description of the consecration of Aaron and his sons to the priestly ministry we read of the beginnings of the sacrificial system as embodied in the Tabernacle worship.

a. (9:1-22) The Offerings. The offerings provide the way by which sinful man may approach the all-holy God. The law of the offerings (Leviticus 1-7), and the establishment of the priesthood (Leviticus 8) were necessary preliminaries to the actual establishment of the Tabernacle as the meeting-place between God and man.

The offerings are presented in a logical order:

(1) Sin Offering. Although washed, clothed, and anointed for service, Aaron had need of that cleansing and atonement typified in the Sin Offering.

(2) Burnt Offering. The Burnt Offering was a symbol of perfect consecration in that the entire sacrifice was consumed in smoke.

(3) Meal Offering. In the Burnt Offering the dedication of one's self may be typified. The Meal Offering adds the dedication of one's toil. Through the atoning blood of Christ, typified in the Sin Offering, the believer is accepted "in the beloved" as to his person and labor.

(4) Peace Offering. With its symbolism of joyous fellowship with God and His people, the Peace Offering comes last in order.

b. (9:23) The Blessing. The Tabernacle service was concluded by the blessing pronounced by Aaron, doubtless in the words of Numbers 6:24-26: "The Lord bless thee and keep thee; the Lord make his face to shine upon thee, and be gracious unto thee; the Lord lift up his countenance upon thee, and give thee peace." From the cloud which rested on the Holy of Holies some new splendor appeared, for we read that "the glory of the Lord appeared unto all the people."

c. (9:24) Fire from Heaven. As an indication of God's acceptance of the sacrifices, a flash of fire suddenly consumed the sacrifices on the altar in the sight of all the people. In like manner God indicated His acceptance of the sacrifices of Gideon (Judges 6:20, 21), Elijah (I Kings 18:28), and of Solomon's sacrifices at the time of the dedication of the Temple (II Chronicles 7:1-2).

3. (10) The Sin and Punishment of Nadab and Abihu. Following the solemn consecration of Aaron and his sons and the beginnings of the ministrations of the Aaronic priesthood, the sin of presumption on the part of Nadab and Abihu resulted in speedy judgment.

a. (10:1) Their Sin. The sin of Nadab and Abihu appears to have been manifold:

　　1. Their incense was not lighted from the altar (cf. 16:12). Thus they offered "strange fire" which was contrary to God's command.

　　2. They appear to have offered the incense at a time not prescribed in the divinely-appointed order of service.

3. Their offering of fire "before the Lord" seems to imply that they pressed "within the veil" into the Holy of Holies where the Shekinah glory of God dwelt. None but the High Priest, and he only once a year on the Day of Atonement, had the right of access to the Holy of Holies (cf. 16:1-2).

b. **(10:2) Their Punishment.** They were instantly killed. Fire "from before the Lord" devoured them.

c. **(10:3) The Warning.** Through Moses, God explained the meaning and significance of His sovereign act in the death of Nadab and Abihu. Those who approach God must come as He wills. Those who have access to God have responsibility as well as privilege.

d. **(10:4-7) Disposal of the Bodies of Nadab and Abihu.** Aaron and his sons were warned against any public display of grief over the death of Nadab and Abihu. The "anointing oil of the Lord" was upon them; hence they represented God and must not question His sovereign act and righteous judgment. Mishael and Elzaphan, sons of Aaron's uncle, were charged with the responsibility of burying Nadab and Abihu.

e. **(10:8-11) Instructions to Aaron and His Sons.** The priesthood is warned against the use of intoxicating beverages in connection with the Tabernacle ministry. An inebriated condition clouds judgment, and removes distinctions between the sacred and profane. The place of this instruction, following the account of the rash act of Nadab and Abihu, has caused many to surmise that they were under the influence of liquor when they committed their acts of sacrilege.

f. **(10:12-21) The Disposal of the Offerings.** In view of the tragic events of the day, Moses gave fresh instructions to Aaron and his sons concerning the sacred offerings, that nothing else might be done in a way different from that which had been prescribed.

Moses was displeased when he noted that the goat of the Sin Offering had been burnt instead of eaten, as had been directed. In anger, Moses demanded an explanation of Eleazar and Ithamar, the priests. Aaron, speaking for his sons, explained that the events of the day (i.e. the death of Nadab and Abihu) had so affected the priests that they deemed themselves unworthy of partaking of the sacred offerings. Moses was content with this explanation.

C.   The Laws of Purity (Chaps. 11-15).

1.   (11) Laws of Clean and Unclean Food. To the Israelite, every detail of life must be governed by the law of God, and lived to the glory of God. In many instances we may not be able to determine the reasons for the prohibitions of certain foods. Some of them were doubtless associated with idolatry. We know that the command not to seethe a kid in its mother's milk (Exodus 23:19, 34:26) is related to the Canaanite practice described in one of the Ugaritic tablets. We are told that horse flesh was deemed sacred to the Germanic god Odin, and was therefore forbidden to the Saxons who became Christians, for fear of a temptation to compromise with older pagan ideals. Many of the Israelite laws regarding clean and unclean foods may have had a similar history.

a.   (11:1-28) The Question Considered from the Standpoint of Diet.

(1)   Quadrupeds (11:2-8). The diet of the Israelite was largely restricted to animals used in sacrifice. Only those which divide the hoof and chew the cud were allowed. The terms are practical, and must not be considered as strictly scientific classifications. The camel, coney, hare, and swine were explicitly forbidden.

(2)   Seafood (11:9-12). Only that seafood which has fins and scales was permitted. Forbidden were eels, shell-fish, lobsters, crabs, oysters, and frogs.

(3)   Birds (11:13-19). Birds of prey are listed as unclean, and thus to be had "in abomination." Doves, pigeons, quails, and sparrows were acceptable in the diet of the Israelite.

(4)   Insects (11:20-23). Most insects were forbidden. Four insects of the locust family (11:22) were permitted. Thus the diet of John the Baptist (Matthew 3:4) conformed to the law.

The temporal nature of the laws of clean and unclean food is evident in the calling of Peter to bring the gospel message to Cornelius. To impress upon the mind of Peter that God had cleansed the Gentile, Cornelius, God caused

Peter to see a vision in which a large sheet was covered with unclean food. When Peter objected to the command, "Rise Peter, kill and eat," the Lord replied, "What God hath cleansed, that call not thou common" (Acts 10:14-16). The question of the responsibility of the Gentile to the observance of dietary laws was the subject of the council convened at Jerusalem (Acts 15). The Gentile church was urged not to abuse its liberty, but it was made clear that the Gentile was not subject to the ceremonial aspects of the Mosaic law.

b. (11:24-42) The Question Considered from the Standpoint of Physical Contact. Uncleanness may be contracted as a result of contact with dead bodies of beasts or creeping things (literally, "swarming things"). An individual so defiled remains ceremonially unclean until evening. If they fall into an earthen vessel, the vessel is to be destroyed. Any food or drink which may be in the vessel into which one of these creatures falls is rendered unclean.

The "swarming things" may not be eaten (11:42). They were looked upon as "detestable things" or "an abomination."

c. (11:43-47) The People of God Must Be Holy. The necessity of holiness is stressed in relation to Israel's particular position as the people of the Lord. Since God delivered Israel from Egyptian bondage, He has certain rights which they must recognize. They may not always understand why His law asserts some animals to be unclean, and certain acts as defiling, but as the people of God they have the responsibility of discerning between the clean and unclean in accord with His revealed will.

2. (12) Laws of Purification after Childbirth. The Mosaic law recognized the sanctity of marriage as divinely ordained. The command, "Be fruitful and multiply," was given in Eden (Gen. 1:28) and renewed after the flood (Genesis 9:1). Fruitfulness was a sign of God's favor, and barrenness considered a reproach (cf. Genesis 30:24).

The ceremonial uncleanness following childbirth is related to the fact that man is a sinful creature. Following the fall, Eve was told that pain and suffering were to accompany motherhood. Human history has been a succession of births in which sinful man begets sinful man. In such a context the law requires ceremonial purification.

The Canaanites, in contrast to Israel, glorified sex by making it the dominant theme of Baal worship. The detailed directions given to Israel concerning sexual matters were to serve as a means of instruction in the necessity for separation from Canaanite attitudes and practices.

a.   (12:1-5) The Period of Ceremonial Uncleanness after Child Birth. After the birth of a son, a woman is regarded as ceremonially unclean for seven days. Following that time the normal activities of life might be resumed, except that she was not permitted to enter the Sanctuary or touch any hallowed thing for a period of forty days. After the birth of a daughter the time was doubled in each case.

b.   (12:6-8) The Offerings Prescribed for Ceremonial Cleansing. At the close of the period of ceremonial uncleanness the law prescribed a lamb for a Burnt Offering, and a young pigeon or turtle-dove for a Sin Offering. In cases of poverty, a second turtle-dove or pigeon might be substituted for the lamb.

Following the birth of Christ, Mary and Joseph presented a pair of turtle doves (Luke 2:24), indicating the poverty of the surroundings in which the Savior was born.

3.   (13-14) Laws Concerning Leprosy. Leprosy as described in the Bible differs from that which was the scourge of medieval Europe and is now known as Hansen's disease, or *Elephantiasis Graecorum*. Skin blemishes and sores which are now termed psoriasis are included in the Hebrew term *tsara'ath*. Conditions of rot in clothing and buildings are described by the same word.

a.   (13:1-46) Examination and its Result. Various forms of skin blemish are noted. These include:
A scab, postule, or blotch similar to eczema (13:2-8).
A white tumor (13:9-18).
A white scab or pink blotch on the scar of a healed boil (13:18-28).
The presence of thin yellow hairs and crusts on the scalp or chin, caused by ring worms (13:29-37).
White blotches, as tetter (13:38-39).
A pink sore on a bald head (13:40-43).

A person pronounced unclean because of leprosy was excluded from the community (13:44-46; cf. Numbers 5:1-2;

II Kings 7:3, 15:5).

In at least one form of "leprosy" the disease reached a
crisis, after which the afflicted might be declared clean
(13:13). The disease came to the surface, formed itself into a
scale which covered the whole body, then dried and peeled
off.

b.   (13:47-59) Leprosy in Clothing and Leather. Patches of
mildew, mould, or fungous growth on linen, woolen, or
leather garments caused them to be treated as leprous. The
priest quarantined the infected garment for seven days, and
then re-examined it. If the discoloration spread, or remained unchanged after washing, the garment was declared
unclean and burned. If, however, the discoloration had
grown fainter, the infected part alone was taken out and
burned, and the rest of the article could, after being washed,
be used again, provided no new spots appeared. This provision was helpful to the poor who could not afford the
loss of an entire garment.

c.   (14:1-32) Cleansing and Restoration of a Leper. The elab-
orate ritual for the cleansing and restoration of the leper
has elements in common with the consecration of the priests
and the rites of the Day of Atonement. When a cleansed
leper wished restoration to his home and the "camp" of
Israel, he was brought to the priest who met him outside
the camp and carefully examined him there. The healed
man was ordered to bring two clean live birds, some cedar
wood, scarlet yarn, and hyssop. One of the birds was killed
over an earthen vessel containing spring water. The other
bird was dipped in the water mixed with blood, together
with the cedar wood, to which the hyssop was fastened with
the scarlet yarn. Thereupon the priest sprinkled the healed
leper seven times with the blood and water, pronounced
him clean, and allowed the bird to fly away as a symbol of
his recovery to health. Having washed his clothes, shaved
his hair, and taken a bath, the former leper was admitted
into the camp, but was not permitted to occupy his own
dwelling for another week.

On the seventh day he repeated the same ablutions, and
on the eighth day the cleansed man presented three lambs
in sacrifice: a male lamb for a Trespass Offering, a ewe for
a Sin Offering, and another male lamb for a Burnt Offering.

In cases of poverty two turtledoves or pigeons might be offered for the Sin and Burnt Offerings, but a ram (14:21) was required for the Trespass Offering.

The oil of the Trespass Offering was used to anoint the right ear, right thumb, and right toe of the cleansed leper (cf. 8:23-24). Oil was then sprinkled by the priest seven times before the Lord, and the remaining oil was poured on the head of the cleansed leper.

This service signified the consecration of the restored leper to the service of God. The leper had been debarred from both the community of Israel and the services of the Sanctuary. His offerings and anointing restored him to an active participation in the life of Israel and the service of the Lord.

d.   (14:33-53) Leprosy in a House. Certain greenish or reddish depressions in the inner walls of a house are termed "leprosy." As in the case of garments, as much of the house as possible was saved after it had been carefully examined by the priest. The ritual for the cleansing of a house was similar to the first stage in the cleansing of an individual.

The form of the rule regarding leprosy in a house indicates that the provision had only future application. During the wilderness wanderings, Israel dwelt in tents. When, however, Israel reached its destination, the land of Canaan, more permanent abodes would be built, and it was to such that the law had reference.

e.   (14:54-57) Conclusion. The law of leprosy has been given in order that men might discriminate between the unclean and the clean. While we may admire the hygiene implied in the prescribed regulations, we must remember that the ceremonial cleanness here discussed pertained to the status of the Israelite in his community. One who is defiled by leprosy cannot take part in the life of the community, including the services at the Sanctuary. Under certain circumstances the priest might declare a leper clean, and it was important that the law applying to such cases be clearly understood.

4.   (15) Sexual Impurities and Cleansings. Both normal and abnormal sexual conditions are here dealt with, with stress on the need for ceremonial purification.

a.   **(15:1-18) Purification of Men.** A natural bodily issue must
be cleansed by bathing, and the person is regarded as "unclean until evening." Abnormal issues required special
treatment. While the issue continued, everything the afflicted
person touched was considered unclean. On the eighth day
after the issue stopped, two turtle-doves or two pigeons were
offered as a Burnt Offering and a Sin Offering for the
afflicted person. Thus the priest made "atonement for him
before the Lord for his issue."

b.   **(15:19-30) Purification of Women.** The treatment parallels
that for men. A woman who had suffered from such an
"issue of blood" for twelve years, and was thus regarded as
ceremonially impure during all that time, touched the hem
of Jesus' garment, saying to herself, "If I may but touch
his garment, I shall be whole." That touch, according to
the law, should have defiled Jesus. Instead, His divine
power brought health and cleansing in response to her
faith. "Jesus turned, and seeing her He said, 'Daughter, be
of good comfort: thy faith hath made thee whole.' And the
woman was made whole from that hour." (Cf. Matthew
9:20-22).

D.   **The Day of Atonement (Chap. 16).** The Day of Atonement
was the most solemn occasion in the Jewish year. Individual
sins had been dealt with previously. Now "all the iniquities
of the children of Israel, and all their transgressions, even
all their sins" are ceremonially atoned for in one solemn act.
Only on this day could the High Priest enter the Holy of
Holies, the place where the glory of the God of Israel was
visibly manifest.

1.   **(16:1-10) Aaron's Preparation.** Before the High Priest could
officiate he must be ceremonially cleansed. No impurity
could be tolerated in the solemn presence of God.

The ornate priestly garments were put aside, and garments of white linen were put on for the services of the day.
The Day of Atonement was a day of humiliation. The
"garments of glory" were inappropriate.

Aaron next offered sacrifices for himself and his family —
a bullock for a Sin Offering, and a ram for a Burnt Offering. Although ceremonially cleansed, the priests of Israel
were sinners and stood in need of atonement.

Then Aaron offered two he-goats for a Sin Offering for the people, and a ram for a Burnt Offering. The two he-goats constitute one offering. Aaron cast two lots upon the goats: "one lot for the Lord and the other for the scapegoat" *(azazel)* (see below, verses 20-22). The goat on which the lot fell "for the Lord" was offered as a Sin Offering. The other was released alive in the wilderness.

2.   (16:11-14) The Sin Offering for the Priests. A bullock was presented for Aaron and the priests. Then a censer full of coals of fire from the altar was taken with sweet incense into the Holy of Holies, "within the veil."

The incense was then placed on the fire so that a cloud of sweet-smelling incense filled the Holy of Holies. The blood of the bullock was sprinkled on the cover of the ark, the mercy seat, seven times.

3.   (16:15-19) The Sin Offering for the People. The goat of the Sin Offering for the people was treated in a way similar to that of the bullock for the priests. Atonement is made for the Holy Place, i.e., the Holy of Holies, "within the veil," because of the uncleanness of the children of Israel. As the Tabernacle is the place where God meets sinful man, it must be ceremonially pure. No taint of the sin of man dare appear in it.

4.   (16:20-22) The Scapegoat. The live goat of the Sin Offering for the people (verses 7 to 10) is now discussed. The priest placed his hands on the head of the live goat, confessing the sins of the people. Ceremonially those sins are transferred to the goat which is released to flee into the wilderness.

Th name of the Scapegoat *(azazel)* is probably derived from a Hebrew root meaning "to remove." Thus the Scapegoat is the goat which depicts the removal of the sins of God's people, just as the goat that is killed in the offering depicts the atoning blood which saves from sin. Both goats form one Sin Offering on the Day of Atonement, expressing related truths.

5.   (16:23-28) The Offerings Completed. After his ministrations in the Tabernacle, Aaron was commanded to lay aside his linen garments and, after bathing, array himself once more in the garments of the high priesthood.

In the outer court, a Burnt Offering was again made "for himself and for the people." The fat of the Sin Offering was burned on the altar. The carcasses of the bullock and goat were taken "without the camp" where the skin, flesh, and dung of the bodies were burned.

6. (16:29-34) The Solemnity of the Day. The law of the Day of Atonement is described as a "statute for ever." The faithful of Israel are reminded of their solemn obligation to observe it year by year. We are reminded that Aaron observed the day at the time of its institution "as the Lord commanded Moses."

II   *Continuance in Communion with God*
(Chaps. 17-26).

A. Holiness on the Part of the People (Chaps. 17-20). The Day of Atonement was instituted to purge, in a special way, the whole of Israel from all their sins, and present them an holy nation before the Lord once a year. The record of its institution is followed by regulations concerning the affairs of the daily life of the people in order to foster the holiness which the God of Israel demands of His people.

1.   (17) Holiness in Regard to Food.

a.   (17:1-9) Every Meal a Sacrifice. When an animal was to be used as food by the Israelite during the wilderness wanderings, he was commanded first to bring it to the door of the Tabernacle and there offer it as a Peace Offering to the Lord. The blood was caught in a bowl by the priest and sprinkled on the ground or poured on the sides of the altar of Burnt Offering. The fat was burned for a "sweet savour to the Lord."

The purpose of this legislation is clearly indicated: "and they shall no more offer their sacrifices unto *serim* after whom they go awhoring" (17:7). Canaanite religion with its sexual orgies constituted a constant temptation to Israel. God made claims on His people's worship and daily life in order to preserve them from the snares of this licentious worship. God demands all the loyalty and worship of His people.

The changed situation of Israel after entering the land of Canaan brought about an abrogation of this provision. Since the central sanctuary would be too far distant for this law to be operative, it was permitted privately to kill and eat clean animals, provided the other aspects of the dietary law were observed (Deuteronomy 12:20-24).

b.   (17:10-14) Prohibition of Blood. As part of the sacrificial offerings, blood was presented to the Lord. As the carrier of life, blood was sacred to God. Under no circumstances was the Israelite, or the stranger who sojourned with him to eat blood.

c.   (17:15-16) Prohibition of Eating Animals not Killed by Man. Animals that die of themselves, presumably of some sickness, and animals killed by other animals may not be eaten. Ceremonial uncleanness results for the one who violates this law. Washing the clothes and bathing the person will restore the transgressor who will be deemed clean the following day.

2.　**(18)** Holiness in the Marriage Relation. Chapters 18-20 are frequently called "The Holiness Code." 18:1-5 forms a preface, and 20:22-26 a solemn conclusion to the section. Chapters 18 and 19 contain the precepts, and chapter 20 states the punishment for the violator.

a.　**(18:1-5)** Impressive Introduction. The commands of this chapter, dealing with marriage relationships, are addressed to all of Israel. The commands are stated in the most absolute form. A warning is given against adherence to the customs of Egypt, or adoption of the customs of Canaan. God's reason for demanding obedience is repeated: "I am the Lord."

b.　**(18:6-19)** Prohibited Marriage Relationships. The general principle is first stated. Marriage to the near-of-kin is forbidden. A detailed list of such relationships illustrates the principle. Among the Egyptians it was common for brothers and sisters to marry. Such sins were practised at Corinth (I Corinthians 5:1).

c.　**(18:20-23)** Prohibition of Sexual Crimes. Certain of these crimes were associated with the Canaanite environment of the Israelites. Others have been practiced in varied societies.

(1)　Adultery — carnal relations with an already married woman **(18:20)**.

(2)　Infant Sacrifice — classed as a sexual crime because of its association with Canaanite worship. Sacred prostitution and infant sacrifice were the two most degrading aspects of Canaanite culture (18:21).

(3)　Sodomy — homosexual relationships **(18:22)**.

(4)　Bestiality — perversion with animals **(18:23)**.

d.　**(18:24-30)** A Solemn Warning. Violation of the standard of morality set forth in these chapters resulted in the humiliation of nations that were guilty of such crimes. God was about to give the land of Canaan to Israel as a possession. The iniquity of the Canaanites had reached the point where the land was about to "vomit" them out. Israel received the solemn warning, however, that her sin would bring swift recompence. The captivities came as the consequence of Israel's failure to heed this solemn warning.

3. **(19) Holiness in Conduct Toward God and Man.** The conduct required of God's people is based on the nature of God Himself: "Ye shall be holy: for I the Lord your God, am holy" (19:2). The regulations prescribed in this chapter are both ceremonial and ethical. They relate to both tables of the Decalogue.

a. **(19:3-8) The First Table of the Law.** The responsibilities of the individual to God comprise the first table of the Law. In a general way these are repeated here.

(1) Honor to Parents **(19:3).** The first unit of society is the family. Through mother and father the child should first come to the knowledge of God.

(2) Sabbath Observance **(19:3).** The Sabbath recognizes God's rights to our time. Sabbath breaking was looked upon as rebellion against God.

(3) Avoiding Idolatry **(19:4).** Much of the history of Israel was tainted with idolatry, and much of the Mosaic law was designed to preserve Israel from its snares. Idolatry was a denial of the God of Israel.

(4) The Peace Offering **(19:5-8).** The Peace Offering was the one offering in which the offerer shared. He must avoid the temptation of taking more than his alloted portion. Any intention to keep the offering beyond the prescribed time renders it unacceptable.

b. **(19:9-18) The Second Table of the Law.** Right relationship with God demands a right relationship to the members of human society. Positive attitudes of love transcend a legalistic concept of righteousness.

(1) Consideration of the Poor **(19:9-10).** The poor and the stranger should be permitted to "glean" from the fields of the Israelite. This principle may be seen in the record of Ruth, the Moabitess, gleaning in the field of Boaz.

(2) Prohibition against Robbery and Deceit **(19:11)**. Robbery, deceit, and falsehood are violations of the Law and expressions of lack of faith in Divine Providence. The Bible clearly recognizes the institution of private property.

(3) Prohibition against False Swearing **(19:12)**. The Name of God is not to be lightly used in taking oaths. While any careless use of the Name of God is against the Law of God, the specific sin here mentioned is that of invoking the Name of God as witness to that which is a falsehood, or calling upon God to bear witness to the truthfulness of that which is a lie! Such swearing usually has as its purpose the defrauding of a neighbor, hence the prohibition in this context.

(4) Prohibition against Oppression **(19:13)**. The employer is warned against taking unfair advantage of the employee. Wages should be paid without delay.

(5) Care for the Helpless **(19-14)**. The deaf and the blind are at the mercy of society. Those who have their faculties shall exhibit godliness in a special concern for the afflicted.

(6) Righteous Judgments **(19:15)**. A corrupt judge is an abomination (cf. Deuteronomy 25:16). Sympathizing with the poor because of his poverty, or favoring the "mighty" because of his wealth or influence, may result in perverted judgments. The one demand of a judge is righteousness.

(7) Warning Against Tale-bearing **(19:16)**. Slander, gossip, and "false witness" are sins against love and demonstrate an attitude of hostility to God and man. Love "rejoiceth not in iniquity" (I Corinthians 13:6).

(8) The Summary of the Second Table of the Law **(19:17-18)**. Negatively, the Israelite is commanded to remove any enmity toward his brother which may be in his heart. Positively, "Thou shalt love thy neighbor as thyself." Jesus referred to this verse when answering the question, "Which is the great commandment of the law?" (Matthew 22:36). In answer to the question, "Who is my neighbor?" He related the parable of the Good Samaritan (Luke 10:29-37).

c. **(19:19-29)** Various Ordinances. The series of ordinances here presented cover a variety of subjects. Some of them are related to the evils of Canaanite religious practices.

(1) Prohibition against "Hybrids" **(19:19)**. At creation each species was told to reproduce "after its kind." Mules in the Old Testament are first mentioned in David's time, and may be regarded as a foreign importation (cf. I Kings 10:25). This law may have been designed to teach the divinely-established order of nature.

(2) The Sin of a Betrothed Bondmaid **(19:20-22)**. In the case of a free woman the sinful relationship here described would have been punished by death for both parties (Deuteronomy 22:23-24). In this case the woman is rather a concubine than a full wife and a lighter penalty is prescribed. Since the rights of the master to whom the woman was espoused are involved, a Trespass Offering is prescribed as a condition of pardon.

That slavery and its attendant ills are here recognized does not imply that they are approved by God. Jesus stated that certain of the Mosaic laws were given because of the hardness of men's hearts (Matthew 19:8). The law restrained evil, but awaited the advent of Christ for the fullest realization of its purposes.

(3) The "First-Fruit" of the Trees of Canaan **(19:23-25)**. Before entering Canaan, Moses gave instruction concerning the planting of trees in the land. Three years after planting the fruit was to be regarded as "uncircumcised" (i.e. like a child who had not been consecrated to the Lord). In the fourth year, when the fruit had matured, it was offered to the Lord as the first-fruits of the trees. In the fifth year the people were permitted to eat the fruit.

(4) Abstention from Heathen Rites **(19:26-29)**. The eating of blood was forbidden not only because blood was sacred to God and the means of atonement, but also because of its association with heathen religious rites. Charms, enchantments, and divination from omens were prohibited. The hair or the beard was not to be cut, in imitation of idolatrous practices. Cuttings of the flesh and tattooing were forbidden for the same reason. Circumcision was the only mark on the body of the obedient Israelite.

As the heathen dedicated their daughters to be temple prostitutes, the command, "Profane not thy daughter, to make her a harlot," has special force. Israel was to be separated by law and life from her idolatrous neighbors.

d. (19:30-37) Closing Injunctions. This section of Leviticus
    closes with a series of injunctions, in part by way of
    repetition, to re-enforce the truths presented.

(1) Honor to the Sabbath and the Sanctuary (19:30). Never a
    matter of empty formalism, true Sabbath observance and
    proper regard for God's House are basic to godliness —
    including correct relations to God and His creatures.

(2) Avoid "familiar spirits" and "wizards" (19:31). Those who
    profess to communicate with the dead and to tell fortunes
    are associated with the heathenism concerning which Israel
    receives solemn warning.

(3) Honor the Aged (19:32). The enthusiasm of youth may have
    little patience with the conservatism of age. Yet the godly
    old person has much to teach inexperienced youth. Honor-
    ing age has its rewards.

(4) Deal Kindly with the Stranger (19:33-34). Israel is asked to
    remember the years of Egyptian bondage. "Ye were strang-
    ers in the land of Egypt," therefore deal righteously with
    the stranger.

(5) The Standard of Righteousness (19:35-36). The measures
    should be the same for buying and selling. Absolute honesty
    is demanded in every aspect of life. Israel was redeemed
    from Egyptian bondage. This privilege brought responsi-
    bility.

(6) Summary (19:37). The reason for absolute obedience is re-
    peated in the words: "I am the Lord." There can be no
    appeal from the Lord Himself.

4. (20) Punishment for Unholiness. The Holiness Code,
    Leviticus 18-20, concludes with a solemn declaration of
    penalties by which the revolting crimes discussed in chapters
    18 and 19 should be punished.

a. (20:1-5) Molech Worship. Molech worship involved the
    sacrifice of children to a Canaanite deity. Excavations in
    Palestine have revealed piles of ashes and vestiges of infant
    skeletons in cemeteries around heathen altars. Molech wor-
    ship was encouraged by Solomon (I Kings 11:7), Manasseh
    (II Kings 21:6), and the kings in the last days of Judah
    (Jeremiah 32:35). Prohibited in the Levitical law, Molech

worship was denounced by Amos (5:26), Jeremiah (7:29-34; 19:1-13), and Ezekiel (16:20-21; 20:26, 31; 23:37-39).

The penalty for causing children to "pass through the fire to Molech" is death. Although severe, the punishment fits the crime.

b. (20:6-8) Consorting with Wizards and Necromancers. In the context of heathen religions, those who profess to contact the dead and control the future are an abomination to the God of Israel. Those who consort with them are subject to the judgment of God.

c. (20:9) Cursing Parents. The cursing of father or mother is both a grievous violation of the law and a denial of the very existence of the family which God ordained for man's good.

d. (20:10-21) Sexual Crimes. The death penalty is pronounced for the sin of adultery (20:10, cf. 18:20); carnal intercourse with a father's wife (20:11, cf. 18:7-8); with a daughter-in-law (20:12, cf. 18:17); sodomy (20:13, cf. 18:22); sexual intercourse with a mother and her daughter (20:14, cf. 18:17); lying with a beast (20:15, 16, cf. 18:23); sexual intercourse with a half-sister (20:17, cf. 18:9, 11); and lying with a menstruous woman (20:18, cf. 18:19).

The means of punishment in these cases was stoning (20:2, 27). In the case of sin with a mother and her daughter, the corpses of the guilty parties were then burned (20:14).

Marriage with an aunt (20:19), with an uncle's wife (20:20), or with a sister-in-law (20:21) is a transgression of God's law, and the guilty parties "shall bear their iniquity." Judgment, however, is left to God. The nation of Israel is not ordered to take direct action in such cases.

e. (20:22-26) Exhortation to Faithfulness. God had brought His people out of Egypt and was about to dispossess the Canaanites, whose cup of iniquity was full. The abominations of Baal and Molech worship were such that God had brought horrible judgment upon its perpetrators. Through God's grace, Israel was given the land. Israel must learn to "separate" or distinguish between the clean and the unclean. The God of holiness had set Israel apart as His peculiar treasure. His rights to His people must not be challenged.

f.   **(20:27)** Warning against Unfaithfulness. In being true to God, Israel must shun every form of idolatry. The mediums who lead the people astray are to be stoned. This sin is high treason against God Himself.

B.   Holiness on the Part of the Priests and Holiness of the Offerings (Chaps. 21-22). As God's representatives, the priests are to be careful to avoid that which is sinful and that which is ceremonially defiling. Following the "Law of Holiness," which was binding on all Israelites, came specific regulations which applied to the priests because of their sacred office.

1.   **(21:1-4)** Contact with a Dead Body. Priests must avoid ceremonial defilement by avoiding contact with a dead body except in cases where there are no other close relatives to perform burial rites. The High Priest must not touch a dead body even in such cases (21:11).

2.   **(21:5-6)** Abstention from Heathen Practices. Because of the fact that the priests have the sacred ministry of offering sacrifices to the God of Israel, particular care must be taken to avoid the heathen attitudes and customs of their neighbors.

3.   **(21:7-8)** Marriage of Priests. Since the priesthood was hereditary, it was expected that priests would marry. The priest must not, however, marry a woman of questionable reputation or a divorcee. The High Priest could not marry a widow (21:14).

4.   **(21:9)** The Family of the Priests. The priest must "rule well his own household." For the daughter of a priest to become a harlot is a particularly heinous offence. Although such sins were common enough in Canaanite fertility cults, they were not to be tolerated in Israel.

5.   **(21:10-15)** The High Priest. The High Priest is subject to the rules for the priesthood but his position of responsibility involves a greater strictness in their application and observance. He is not permitted to defile himself even for the purpose of the burial of his father or mother. At such a time he must not leave the Sanctuary (21:12) but continue in the performance of his priestly ministry. He may marry

only a virgin. To violate the marriage law would unfit his children for the priestly office.

6. **(21:16-24) Priests with Physical Blemishes.** As the offerings presented in the sanctuary had to be without blemish, so the ministering priests must be free of bodily blemishes. Priests who were disqualified from ministering in the Tabernacle because of physical blemishes were, however, supported by the offerings of the people and permitted to eat of the priest's portion of the offerings.

7. **(22:1-10) Priestly Separation from Ceremonial Uncleanness.** A ceremonially unclean member of the priesthood dare not partake of the "holy things," i.e. that part of the offerings designated for the priests and termed "most holy."

Ceremonial impurity in the priesthood is similar to that among the laity. It may result from leprosy, a bodily issue, touching a dead body, contact with a living person who is ceremonially unclean, or contact with unclean creeping things or animals.

The priestly portion of the sacrifices was to be preserved for those priests who were ceremonially clean, and no others dare partake of the priest's portion.

8. **(22:11-16) The Rights of the Priest's Family to the "Holy Things."** Persons not belonging to the immediate family of the priest were excluded. An exception was made in the case of a slave purchased by a priest and reckoned a member of his family (22:11). A married daughter of a priest was excluded unless, because of being widowed or divorced, she returned to her father's house (22:12-13).

If "holy things" were eaten by mistake, the guilty party was to make restitution to the priests, adding a fifth as in the Trespass Offering.

9. **(22:17-33) Vows and Freewill Offerings.** All sacrifices, whether made by Israelites or non-Israelites ("strangers in Israel" 22:18), must be without blemish. Nothing but perfect specimens should be offered to God.

The animal sacrificed must be at least eight days old, and in no case should the mother and its young be sacrificed on the same day. The young animal did not attain to a mature and self-sustained life during its first week, hence the requirement that it be at least eight days old.

Thanksgiving sacrifices must be eaten on the day on which they were offered. The slaughtering of the sacrifice must be performed with this in mind. Whatever is not eaten is burned on the altar.

The purpose of the legal regulations and prescriptions is repeated in the words, "I am the Lord Who sanctifies you." Failure to obey His Law is to profane His Name.

C. Sanctification of Feasts (Chaps. 23-25).

1. (23) Sabbaths and Annual Feasts. The sacred seasons of the Hebrew calendar are indicated by two Hebrew words. The term *mo'ed* is rendered "set feast" or "appointed season" by the Revised Version, "appointed feast" in the Revised Standard Version of the English Bible. It is a general term which applies to all of the sacred seasons.

Three of these sacred seasons are termed *hag*, "feast," a term indicative of special joy and festivity. The feasts of Passover, Pentecost, and Tabernacles are so designated, and every able-bodied male Israelite was enjoined to appear before the Lord at the Sanctuary for their observance (Exodus 23:17; Deuteronomy 16:16).

a. (23:1-3) The Sabbath. The first and most basic of the appointed seasons was the weekly Sabbath. All labor was forbidden. It marked the rest of God following the six creative days (Genesis 2:3) and reminded Israel of its deliverance from Egyptian slavery (Deuteronomy 5:15).

The Sabbath was a sign of Israel's peculiar covenant relation to the Lord (Exodus 31:13). Its observance marked Israel as God's people and served as a reminder of the rest into which God desired to bring them. The generation that left Egypt perished in the wilderness because of unbelief. Although Joshua brought Israel into Canaan, Hebrews 4 reminds us that the rest which God has for His people was not realized by the occupying of Canaan, but was, in its fullest sense, to be realized through the Person and Work of Christ.

b. (23:4-14) Passover and the Feast of Unleavened Bread. The first feast *(hag)* of the Hebrew year was the Passover with the closely related Feast of Unleavened Bread. The Passover celebrated the deliverance from Egypt which marked the beginning of the national life of the Israelites.

On the night of the first Passover a lamb had been slain and blood sprinkled on the lintels and door posts of each Israelite home in the land of Egypt. The families of Israel gathered together to feed on their lambs. Not waiting for bread to be leavened, they prepared, by divine direction, to escape in haste (Exodus 12).

The annual Passover observance included the eating of "bitter herbs" as a reminder of the oppressions of Egyptian bondage, and unleavened bread, reminiscent of the hasty departure from Egypt.

The Feast of Unleavened Bread began on the day after Passover and continued for a week. In preparation for the feast, the Israelite was commanded to sweep out his house in order that no trace of leaven might be found there. In I Corinthians 5:7-8, Paul applies this ancient regulation to the Christian: "Purge out therefore the old leaven, that ye may be a new lump, as ye are unleavened. For even Christ our passover is sacrificed for us."

During the Feast of Unleavened Bread "on the morrow after the sabbath" a "sheaf of first-fruits" of barley was offered as a wave-offering before the Lord. Oil and frankincense were mixed with flour and the whole offered as a meal offering. In waving the sacrifice, i.e. holding it out toward the altar, and bringing it back again, God was recognized as the author of the entire harvest. The harvest was ceremonially dedicated to Him. It was then received back, symbolizing the fact that the blessing of the harvest had come from Him. A portion was burned on the altar, and the rest was eaten by the worshipper.

c.   (23:15-22) Pentecost. Seven weeks were counted after the sheaf of first-fruits of barley had been "waved before the Lord." On the fiftieth day the Feast of Pentecost, or Weeks (*shavu'oth*) was observed. As an agricultural feast, Pentecost celebrated the completion of the wheat harvest. A Meal Offering in the form of two wave loaves baked with leaven was offered. Such loaves constituted the daily food of the people, and the offering implied the consecration of the daily food of God's people. Burnt, Sin, and Peace Offerings were part of the observance of Pentecost.

Since Pentecost marked the end of the grain harvests, the responsibility of the Israelite to leave gleanings in his field for the poor and the stranger was stressed.

d. **(23:23-25)** The Feast of Trumpets. The seventh month was the most sacred in the Hebrew year. The Day of Atonement came on the tenth day of the month. The Feast of Tabernacles was observed on the fifteenth day.

The first day of the seventh month was observed as the Feast of Trumpets, which coincides with the beginning of the civil year. The Feast of Trumpets thus became the Jewish New Year. It should be remembered that the "religious" year began in the spring, the "civil" year began in the fall of the year.

The sounding of trumpets announced the day which was observed by a "holy convocation" and the offering of appropriate sacrifices. Unnecessary work was avoided, and the time was one of great festivity.

e. **(23:26-32)** The Day of Atonement. The ritual of the solemn Day of Atonement was set forth in detail in Leviticus 16. Here it is mentioned in its sequence with the other sacred seasons.

On the Day of Atonement all work was suspended and a "holy convocation" was observed. It was a time of "affliction of soul" and observance of those typical rites which set forth the removal of the sins of a believing people.

f. **(23:33-44)** The Feast of Tabernacles. From the fifteenth to the twenty-second day of the seventh month the Israelites dwelt in tents, or booths, and observed the most joyful feast of the year.

The Feast of Tabernacles was called the Feast of Ingathering and finds its counterpart in our Thanksgiving Day. It marked the end of the agricultural year. The harvests of grain, the produce of vine and fruit tree had all been harvested. The first and eighth days of the feast were marked by "holy convocations" with the offering of appropriate sacrifices.

In addition to the harvest aspect of the Feast of Tabernacles, it served to commemorate the faithfulness of God toward His people during the years of the wilderness wandering. During the days when the Israelites sojourned in tents enroute from Egypt to Canaan they were unable to plant seed and harvest crops, yet God had provided them with manna from heaven and water from the rock. As the

Passover commemorated the beginning of that experience, so the Feast of Tabernacles recalled the experience itself. The Passover and the Feast of Tabernacles provided an annual re-enacting of the experiences of Israel's past as a reminder to future generations of the faithfulness of God, and of their responsibility to Him.

2.   **(24:1-9) Holy Lamps and Shewbread.**

a.   **(24:1-4) The Holy Lamp.** Light was provided for the Holy Place in the Tabernacle by the golden "candlestick" or lampstand. The "candlestick" consisted of a central shaft which supported six branches. Pure beaten olive oil was used for the lamps (cf. Exodus 27:20). Oil was one of the freewill offerings of the people at the time the Tabernacle was constructed, and the people evidently continued to provide it as a freewill offering.

Aaron and his sons (Exodus 27:21) were charged with tending the lamps. According to I Samuel 3:3 it appears that the lamps were lighted in the evening with fire from the altar of Burnt Offering and provided with sufficient fuel to last until morning. Others interpret the term "continually" (24:2) as implying that the lamp burned day and night.

b.   **(24:5-9) The Shewbread.** Opposite the golden candlestick in the Holy Place was the table of shewbread, described in Exodus 25:23-30. The term "shewbread" is, literally, *bread of the presence,* i.e. God's presence. Just beyond the veil which separated the Holy Place from the Holy of Holies, was the throne room of the God of Israel, where His glory was manifest above the Mercy Seat. We may think of the Holy Place as the ante-room of the Palace of the King — as close as anyone could approach the all-holy God of Israel, except for the one occasion during the year when the High Priest might enter the Holy of Holies.

Twelve loaves of shewbread were to be prepared each week. Each loaf consisted of two-tenths of an ephah of flour, or about six quarts. The loaves were probably prepared with oil, like the Meal Offering, but this it not stated. The loaves were placed in two rows (literally, arrangements), six in each row on the table. With (rather than on) each row, frankincense was placed, perhaps in a bowl. The Jewish commentator, Rashi, states the tradition that the frankincense was burned when the shewbread was removed from the golden table each Sabbath. Since none of the bread was offered up to God, the frankincense thus would serve as a "memorial" for the shewbread.

Each Sabbath day, as fresh loaves of shewbread were placed on the table, Aaron and his sons had the privilege of eating those that had been removed.

The twelve loaves of shewbread represented the twelve tribes of Israel. Their place, on the golden altar in the Holy Place, is reminiscent of the standing which Israel had as a people particularly near to Him.

Both the oil for the lamp and the fine flour for the shewbread are offerings to God. Certain portions of the olives and grain of the land were to be dedicated to the sacred ministry of the Holy Place.

3.   **(24:10-23)** Historical: Punishment of a Blasphemer. The historical parenthesis forms an integral part of the book because it provides the occasion for an answer to two questions: (1) What should be the penalty for blasphemy? (2) Should the same penalty apply to Israelites and non-Israelites?

The half-Israelite, whose father was an Egyptian, quarreled with a man of Israel. In the heat of argument he blasphemed the Name of the God of Israel. He was put "in ward," i.e., in the place set aside for offenders, until the will of the Lord in the matter might be revealed.

Moses declared that the penalty for blasphemy was death, and that this should apply to stranger and home-born alike.

Occasion was taken to mention other laws that apply to both stranger and "home-born" Israelite — laws relating to murder, killing a neighbor's beast, and injuring a neighbor.

The principle here declared is known as the *lex talionis,* "an eye for an eye, a tooth for a tooth." Jesus referred to these words in condemning an attitude of personal retaliation and revenge (Matthew 5:38-42). Private irresponsible retaliation was not permitted by the Mosaic law. The *lex talionis* was designed as a principle of exact justice, not revenge. It was publicly administered. It is probable that compensation for injuries usually took the form of a fine. The fact that murder is excluded from the crimes for which ransom is permissible (Numbers 35:31-32) tends to bear this out.

The *lex talionis* may be one of those statutes given through Moses because of the hardness of men's hearts. The strict justice of "an eye for an eye" may serve as a check on the extreme of "a life for an eye." The punishment was made to fit the crime, but not to exceed it.

4.   **(25) Sabbatical and Jubilee Years.**

a.   **(25:1-7) The Sabbatical Year.** The principle of one day of rest in seven is extended to the establishment of a Sabbatical year in which the land is to lie fallow for one year in seven. No holy convocations are mentioned for the Sabbatical year. Labor other than that which was strictly agricultural was permitted. Cessation from agricultural work provided the opportunity for special emphasis on teaching and training Israel in the truths of God's law (Deuteronomy 31:10-13).

That which grew without cultivation during the Sabbatical year was not to be harvested but left for the free use of all. This served as a reminder that the fields ultimately belonged to God. He had the right to dispose of them as He willed, and He could be trusted to provide for the needs of His people during the year their lands were idle. As in the provision for gleaning, so in the Sabbatical year, provision is made for the poor of the land.

b.   **(25:8-55) The Year of Jubilee.** After seven cycles of Sabbatical years, the fiftieth year was celebrated as a Year of Jubilee. The ram's horn *(shophar)* was blown on the Day of Atonement to "proclaim liberty throughout the land unto all the inhabitants thereof."

(1)   Rules for Observance of the Jubilee (25:8-22). The laws concerning sowing and reaping which applied to the Sabbatical Year applied also to the Jubilee. The special significance of the Jubilee Year was its provision for a return of people (slaves) and possessions to their original condition. Property reverted to the original owner at the Jubilee Year. Transfers of property between Jubilee years were made in the light of this provision. When such were made they were really leased for a longer or shorter time, depending upon the closeness of the Jubilee year, and financial arrangements were made accordingly. Thus land could not be permanently alienated from its original owner,

no matter how impoverished he might become. No matter what his financial condition, it reverted to him or his heirs at the Jubilee. The land rightly belongs to God, and His people are reckoned as "strangers and settlers" with Him.

Answer is made to the objection, "What shall we eat the seventh year?" God's blessing will rest upon the obedient people and their land so that there shall be abundance for the Sabbatical and Jubilee years.

(2) The Law of Redemption (25:23-34). It is the responsibility of a near kinsman to redeem the possession of his brother. If the man who in a time of extremity sold a possession later acquired the means of redeeming it himself, he was at liberty to do so, and his right of redemption was protected by law. In the event that no kinsman had been able to redeem the land, and the former owner was unable to do so, it remained alienated until the Jubilee Year.

The custom is illustrated in the book of Ruth. Naomi had a claim to a piece of land in Bethlehem-Judah. Ruth, the widow of her son Elimelech, likewise had a claim. In their poverty neither Ruth nor Naomi could redeem the land. Boaz, a kinsman of Naomi, exercised his right of redemption of the land and also married Ruth.

(3) Treatment of the Poor (25:35-55). The Israelites are to treat one another as brethren, and help one another in need without expectation of reward. When money or food are loaned, no interest is to be exacted. All Israel is in covenant with God, and the land and all its blessings are a trust from Him.

When in dire poverty an Israelite sells himself to another, he is to be treated as a hired servant, not as a slave. At the Year of Jubilee he will be free to return to his own family.

If a poor Israelite sells himself to a wealthy non-Israelite in the land, the Israelite may be redeemed by a kinsman. The non-Israelite is treated fairly and compensated in proportion to the number of years remaining before the Jubilee, when the Israelite would regain his freedom in any event.

Note that the non-Israelite is subject to the law of the land which guarantees the Israelite his liberty at the Year of Jubilee. The non-Israelite may be reduced to perpetual slavery, but the Israelite is preserved by law from the slave status.

D. Conclusion: Promises and Warnings (Chap. 26).

1. **(26:1-2)** The Necessity of Right Relationship to God. The faithful in Israel are commanded to avoid all forms of idolatry, to observe the Lord's sabbaths, and to reverence the Lord's sanctuary. These verses form a summary of man's obligation to God.

2. **(26:3-13)** The Blessings of Obedience to God. The Lord declares Himself to be the sovereign over all the forces of nature, and able to use them in accomplishing His purposes. He delights in blessing His people. His blessings are conditional, however: "If ye walk in my statutes and keep my commandments, and do them." Abundant crops, victory over enemies, a state of peace, large families, and the presence and blessing of God Himself follow an attitude of loving obedience to the Law.

3. **(26:14-39)** The Chastisements for Disobedience. God is a God of holiness, and the violator of His law has judgment resting upon him. The disobedient nation would not only miss the rewards of obedience, but suffer pestilence (26:16, 25), famine (26:19), wild beasts (26:22), and the sword, as emblematic of war and desolation (26:25-39). The intensity of the suffering is suggested by the idiomatic use of the expression "seven times" or, better, "sevenfold" (26:18, 21, 24, 28). The desolations which accompanied the destruction of Jerusalem by the armies of Nebuchadnezzar may be thought of as a graphic illustration of these verses.

4. **(26:40-45)** God's Faithfulness to His Covenant. Although God will surely chasten his rebellious people, He does not utterly cast them off. When they repent of their sin, God remembers His covenant with Abraham, Isaac, and Jacob. They are delivered from their enemies. This principle is repeatedly illustrated in the book of Judges. In days of prosperity, Israel forsook God and adopted the idolatrous practices of the heathen. Thereupon enemy nations oppressed Israel until, in despair, Israel cried out unto God for deliverance. He heard their prayers and raised up a judge who brought military victory. Prosperity, however, brought its temptations, and Israel forgot God, lapsed into idolatry, and the round of chastisement, repentance, and deliverance was repeated. It may also be illustrated by the

events of the Babylonian exile. While the exile was a punishment brought on by the idolatry of God's people, it was
also a means of preserving a faithful remnant who confessed
and forsook their sins. God proved Himself faithful in
bringing them back to their land where, in the fulness of
time, the Savior was born in whom the Levitical offerings
found their ultimate fulfillment.

5.   (26:46) Summary Statement. This group of laws, promises,
     and warnings is concluded with the emphatic statement
     that they were revealed by God to Moses at Mt. Sinai. Be-
     cause of their divine origin, and the solemnity of the
     occasion when they were delivered, they demand the
     utmost respect.

III *Appendix: Concerning Vows* (Chap. 27).

Vows were purely voluntary, but when once made they were considered binding.

1. **(27:2-8)** Vows of Persons. A godly Israelite might wish to dedicate himself or his children to the Lord's service. Priests and Levites ordinarily cared for the religious needs of the community so that it was unnecessary for others to personally serve in Tabernacle or Temple. The vow of dedication was normally discharged by paying into the sanctuary treasury the value of the services covered by the vows.

    The amount to be paid was fixed by the law. Variations were made depending on the sex and the age of the individual. Special provision was made for the poor who might wish to offer themselves in a vow.

2. **(27:9-13)** Vows of Domestic Animals. When the vow was of an animal that could be used for sacrifice, the animal was brought to the sanctuary. Unclean animals were sold and the proceeds devoted to the sanctuary. The person who made the vow might choose to keep the animal and pay its estimated value, plus an additional fifth.

3. **(27:14-25)** Vows of Houses and Fields. When an Israelite wished to present his house for the Lord's service, a priest was asked to estimate its value. The man might continue to live in the house, but apparently he paid rent on the basis of the priest's evaluation. If he wished to redeem it he paid the priest's evaluation, plus an additional fifth.

    An inherited field was evaluated by the priest according to the amount of seed required for sowing the field. If the vow went into effect following the Jubilee Year, the full price had to be paid in redeeming the property. If later, proportional reductions were made. In any cases, one fifth was added to the estimated value of the field.

    Land acquired by purchase was subject to different regulations, for it would revert to the original owner at the next Jubilee Year. Its valuation was determined by the crops it would be expected to produce before the Jubilee. Full, immediate payment was required.

4. **(27:26-33)** Exclusions from the Vows. That which belonged to the Lord by law was not subject to voluntary dedication. Such included:

a. **(27:26-27)** Firstlings Among Beasts. Firstlings belonged to the Lord (Exodus 13:11-15). They could be redeemed, and the value given to the Sanctuary.

b. **(27:28-29)** Devoted Things. Things devoted, or put "under the ban" *(herem)* were considered God's rightful property. They could not be redeemed. A banned person was to be put to death. Such a ban was placed on Amalek and on Jericho. Achan's sin consisted in taking that which was to be "devoted" to the Lord, and determining to make private use of it. The "ban" must be thought of as God's righteous act in judging a people who had wilfully sinned against Him to the point of incorrigibility.

c. **(27:30-33)** The Tithe. The tithe belonged to the Lord. It might be redeemed, however, provided a fifth was added to the article redeemed. It should be remembered that the tithe was not limited to money. Flocks and herds were tithed. Each tenth animal that "passeth under the rod" was to be reckoned as the Lord's. Any manipulation so as to deprive the Lord of the best of the flock was unlawful.